The Island Everyone Wanted

An Illustrated History of Cyprus

By Marina Christofides

Illustrated by Eleni Lambrou

ISBN 978-1-7238571-0-2
© Marina Christofides

Published by: Verity Productions
Design & Supervision of production: Marcia Dallas
Computer work: Electra Chamatilla
Colour separation: Laser Graphics
Printed by Kailas Press
Nicosia, Cyprus, November 2007.

Contents

4-5	Map
6-7	**Ancient Times**
8-9	Millions of years ago
10-11	The stone village
12-13	Copper Island
14-15	City kingdoms
16-17	King Evagoras of Salamis
18-19	The Ptolemies
20-21	Roman province
22-23	A new religion
24-25	**The Middle Ages**
26-27	Byzantine outpost
28-29	Arab raids
30-31	Richard the Lionheart
32-33	French kings and queens
34-35	Venetian stronghold
36-37	**Modern Times**
38-39	Ottoman rule
40-41	British colony
42-43	Independence
44-45	Coup, invasion and a plan for peace
46-47	Chronology

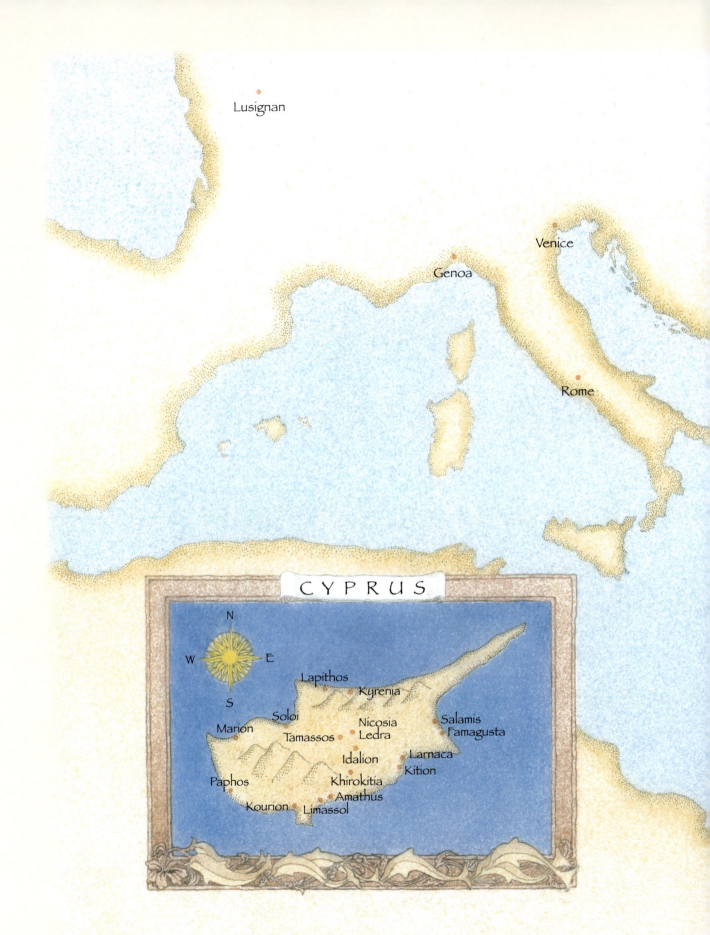

Ancient Times

Millions of years ago

Long before there were any humans in this world, the land which is now the island of Cyprus was at the bottom of the Mediterranean Sea. Over the years the sea floor was squeezed and pushed until it rose out of the water, a small knot of land, like a belly button, in the centre of the world. The first parts to appear were the Troodos and Kyrenia mountains. Later, they were joined up by the Mesaoria plain. Cyprus is one of the few places in the world where scientists can come and study the ocean bed without getting wet.

In the olden days Cyprus was lush and green and covered in forests. It had rivers and streams. The first animals in Cyprus were pygmy hippopotami and elephants that swam all the way here from the surrounding lands about one and a half million years ago. Apart from some shrews and mice, these were the only animals roaming the island before man arrived about ten thousand years ago.

The stone village

The very first signs of humans in Cyprus were found in caves by the sea and date back 10,000 years. They may have been living there permanently or they may have been hunting parties from nearby lands just passing through.

At around 6000 BC people started to live together in villages. One of the oldest is Khirokitia. The ruins of the village, which is halfway between Nicosia and Limassol, can be seen today on a hill on the banks of a river.

About 300 people lived there in round flat-roofed houses built of stones and other material which they collected from the surrounding hills and from the riverbed. The houses formed groups of huts around an open courtyard, like rooms - some were used for cooking and eating others for sleeping and still others for storing things. A wall of stones surrounded the whole village for protection.

These stone-age Cypriots were hunters and farmers and they used stones for everything - for weapons and tools, plates and cups, even for jewellery. They grew cereal crops and vegetables and picked fruit from trees that grew nearby, like nuts, figs, olives and plums. They kept sheep, goats and pigs and hunted deer and wild boar and went fishing. They even had pet cats, the oldest skeleton of which has been found here buried near its owner. People in those days died young and the dead were buried under the floors of the houses.

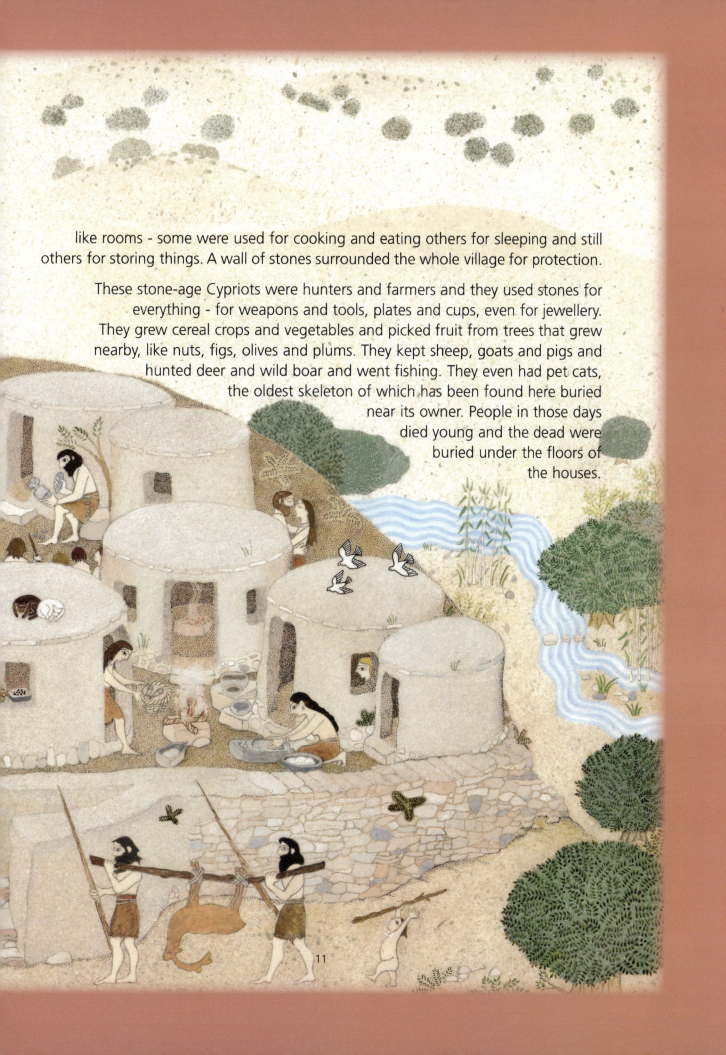

Copper Island

When copper was discovered in Cyprus in 2500 BC, the island became rich and famous. The metal - *cuprum* in Latin - may even have been named after the island. Copper was melted to make it pure and given a shape like an ox-hide to make it easy to carry. These copper ingots were used for trade and mostly exported.

Cyprus' location and its wealth from copper brought traders and settlers to the island. Mycenaean and Achaean Greeks came bringing their culture, language and art.

They also taught Cypriots all about their gods. One goddess in particular, the goddess of fertility, Aphrodite, was worshipped here, especially in Paphos. Cyprus became her special island and temples were built for her in beautiful spots on top of cliffs.

Greeks were not the only people to settle in Cyprus. From the neighbouring coast of what today is Lebanon, came people called Phoenicians. They were excellent traders and settled mainly in Kition near today's Larnaca, just across the water from their homeland.

City kingdoms

A number of city kingdoms were established on the island. These were like tiny separate countries and there were about ten in all – Kyrenia, Lapithos, Soloi, Marion, Paphos, Kourion, Amathus, Kition, Idalion and Salamis.

The island also attracted a long sequence of foreign masters - the Assyrians, the Egyptians and then the Persians. All the great powers of the time wanted to rule Cyprus. Mostly these conquerors allowed the city kingdoms to rule themselves as long as they paid taxes to the new rulers.

In 498 BC all the kingdoms of Cyprus, except Amathus, joined with the people of Ionia, a Greek land which had also been conquered by the Persians, in revolt against Persian rule.

They were led by Onesilus, king of Salamis. The Persians landed near Salamis and there was a fierce battle. The king of Kourion betrayed them and they were defeated. Onesilus was killed.

King Evagoras of Salamis

The Ionian revolt brought Cyprus into the fight between two important powers - Greece and Persia. When it was suppressed, Persia stayed firmly in control.

Cyprus tried to get rid of the Persians again in the 4th century BC with King Evagoras of Salamis. He had the vision of uniting all the city kingdoms under his leadership. He wanted to create close ties with the Greek states. He promoted Greek culture,

introduced the Greek alphabet and issued coins of Greek design. Most of the other kings joined him except three – those of Kition, Amathus and Soloi. They turned to the Persians for help, while Evagoras turned to the Athenians and later the Egyptians. However, they abandoned him and he was defeated and eventually murdered.

Cyprus stayed in Persian hands until Alexander the Great defeated the Persian Empire and took over. Then Cyprus became part of Alexander's empire.

The Ptolemies

Alexander ruled Cyprus for only ten years. After he died in 323 BC his heirs fought over his empire. Eventually one of his generals, Ptolemy I, who had taken control of Egypt, also took over Cyprus. Cyprus was ruled by Ptolemy and his family as part of the Hellenistic Kingdom of Egypt for 200 years

The Ptolemies moved the capital from Salamis to Paphos because it was nearer Egypt. It had rich forests providing plenty of wood for ship building and a fine harbour from where Cypriots sailed the seas selling their wares in competion even with the Phonoecians. A small Greek merchant ship, which sunk off the coast of Kyrenia at

around this time and was discovered in 1965, shows us how important Cyprus was for trading. The ship carried goods from different islands of the Mediterranean - wine from Rhodes, millstones from Nisyros and even thousands of almonds, which had probably just been collected from Cyprus and were still perfectly preserved in hundreds of amphorae.

The Ptolemies abolished the city kingdoms and established a central administration. They introduced the *demos*, or parliament, with its *house* and *senate*, as well as the *gymnasium* where young men trained to be fit and healthy.

Roman Province

When the Ptolemy brothers started quarrelling with each other, Rome, the great power of the time, found an excuse to conquer Cyprus and expand her empire. At first Rome governed the island as part of the province of Cilicia. Cicero, the famous orator, was governor. Later it was ruled directly from Rome and governed by a proconsul whose seat was in Paphos.

In 40 BC the Roman general, Mark Anthony, gave Cyprus to Cleopatra, the Queen of Egypt, as a present in token of his love. When he and Cleopatra committed suicide ten years later, Cyprus was transferred back to Rome.

During Roman rule Cyprus enjoyed 300 years of peace. The island flourished, especially Salamis, which became a centre of culture, education and commerce. When an earthquake destroyed it in 15 BC, the Emperor Augustus had it rebuilt in the grand Roman fashion of the time. Salamis was shattered by an earthquake again in the fourth century. After it was rebuilt it was renamed Constantia and became the capital of the island once more.

Most of the ancient ruins you can see in Cyprus today are from the Roman time - gymnasia, theatres, public baths. The Romans made sure that all the cities of Cyprus had a good water supply and were linked by roads.

Many houses of this time had beautiful floors decorated with mosaics, which were pictures made out of tiny coloured stones showing scenes from Greek mythology.

A new religion

Christianity was introduced to the island during Roman times. It all started in 45 AD when the Apostle Paul came to Cyprus on his first mission to spread the new religion. He was accompanied by the Apostle Barnabas, a native of Salamis and a Greek Jew.

The two missionaries travelled from Salamis across the island to Paphos, preaching and making converts. There, according to tradition, Paul was tied to a column and flogged.

When the Roman proconsul in Paphos, Sergius Paulus, heard about them, he invited them to visit him. A sorcerer, Elymas, was also there and challenged the Apostles. This angered Paul who turned him blind. Sergius Paulus thought this was a miracle and decided to convert to Christianity, making Cyprus the first country in the world to be ruled by a Christian. Before the two Apostles left the island, they set up the Church of Cyprus, one of the oldest independent churches in the world.

The Middle Ages

Byzantine Outpost

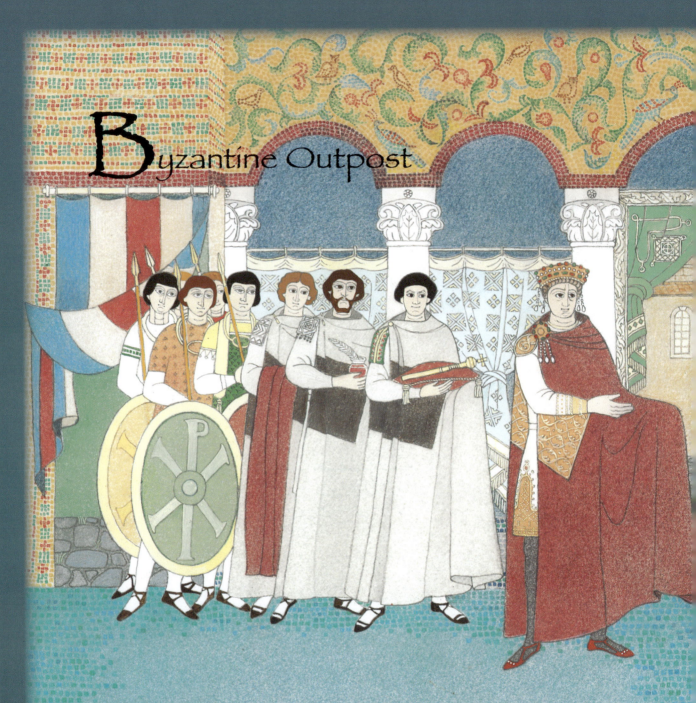

When the Roman Empire was split in two, Cyprus became part of the Byzantine Empire, whose capital was Constantinople, and was governed by rulers sent by the Byzantine Emperor.

A number of people involved in the beginnings of the Church of Cyprus were sanctified and the island became known as "the island of saints". One of them was Lazarus, who was believed to have been brought back from the dead by Jesus. He came to Cyprus and became bishop of Kitium. St Helena once visited Cyprus and brought with her pieces of the Holy Cross on which Jesus was crucified. She left these at Stavrovouni monastery, which she founded, and at Tohni, where they are still kept today.

The Church of Cyprus tried to stay independent from the leading Byzantine church of Antioch in Constantinople and succeeded when the Archbishop of Cyprus, Anthemios, managed to convince the Byzantine Emperor that the church of Cyprus was founded by Apostles.

It has since remained autocephalous and the Archbishop was given special rights - he carries a sceptre instead of a shepherd's staff, wears a red cloak and signs his name in red ink.

A church was built over St Barnabas' grave, one of many beautiful churches built in the Byzantine period. They had domed roofs, mosaics and paintings on the walls.

Arab raids

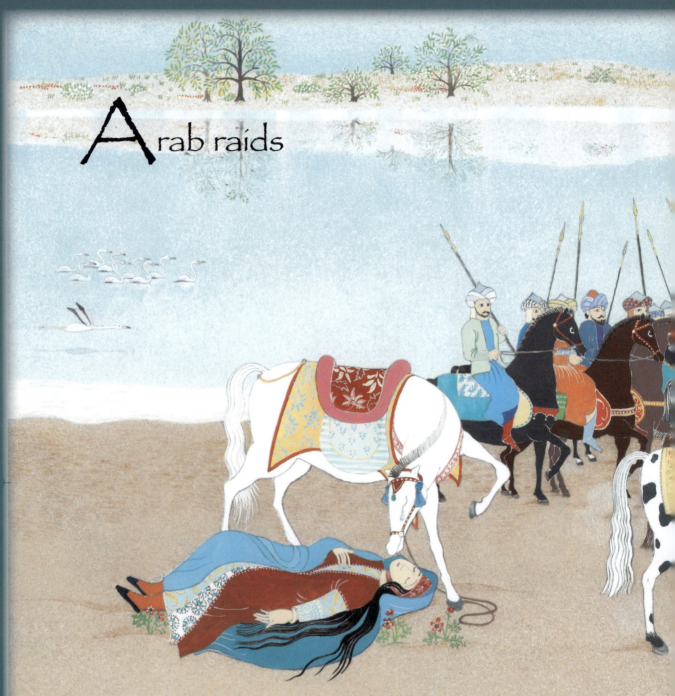

Another new religion started to develop in nearby Arab lands in the 7th century. It was called Islam and followed the teachings of the Prophet Mohammed.

The Arabs became a great power and attacked many lands of the Byzantine Empire. It was hoped the sea would keep Cyprus safe, but the Arabs built a fleet of ships and landed at Constantia - Salamis. They then rode across the island killing many people and destroying many places as they went.

To defend themselves from the Arab raids the people built castles. Three large ones were built in the Kyrenia mountains along the north coast - Buffavento, St Hilarion and Kantara. They were perched high on mountaintops so they could keep a

lookout for miles around. Legend has it that during one of these raids, Umm-Haram, one of the wives of an Arab commander, who was said to be related to the Prophet, fell off her horse near the Larnaca salt lake and died. A mosque, the Hala Sultan Tekke, was built at the spot where she was buried and is one of the holiest places in the Moslem world.

Eventually the Byzantine Emperor, Nicephorus Phocas, sent troops to Cyprus to put an end to the Arab raids. After the devastation of the coastal cities, the capital was moved inland to Nicosia, built on the ruins of an older city called Ledra. The governors who were sent to Cyprus were now called Dukes.

Richard the Lionheart

One day in 1191 three ships arrived off the coast of Limassol carrying two very important ladies - Queen Joanna of Sicily and Berengaria of Navarre, who was engaged to be married to the King of England, Richard the Lionheart.

They had all set sail from England to go to the Holy Land as part of the Third Crusade, which was a war to liberate Jerusalem from the Arabs. However, a storm had struck and scattered the fleet.

The ruler of Cyprus, Isaac Comnenus, had tried to trick the women into coming ashore so he could hold them for ransom. King Richard arrived just in time and spoiled his plan.

Richard married Berengaria in the chapel of St. George in Limassol. The next day the rest of the English fleet arrived. Isaac ran away and hid in Kantara castle, hoping Richard would go away. But Richard fell ill and stayed in Cyprus.

A Frenchman named Guy de Lusignan, who was Richard's friend, took over the army and marched on the castle. Isaac surrendered, asking only that he should not be chained in irons. So they chained him in silver instead.

Richard stayed on the island for only a year, finding it useful for storing ammunition and organising expeditions to the Holy Land. But soon he found it too troublesome to keep because the people kept on revolting. So when he no longer had any use for it, he sold it, first to the Knights Templars, who later sold it back to him, and then eventually to his friend, Guy de Lusignan.

French kings and queens

This was a period of 300 years when European royalty ruled Cyprus along the feudal model. They all spoke French and were the family and descendants of the Frenchman, Guy de Lusignan.

The kings, queens, princes, nobles, barons and knights of the Kingdom of Cyprus were all very rich and lived a life of luxury. Their favourite pastime was hunting moufflon and leopards. The kings and queens lived in the old Byzantine castles and made them bigger and better, such as those of Nicosia, Paphos, Limassol, Kyrenia, St. Hilarion, Buffavento and Kantara.

They used the largest, St Hilarion, as a summer palace. It had a beautiful view, especially from the Queen's bedroom. They used Buffavento as a lookout and a prison for the king's enemies. They also built gothic churches and and other beautiful buildings of their own, such as Bellapais Abbey, St. Sophia Cathedral and Kolossi castle.

King Peter I is the best known of the Kings of Cyprus. People still sing songs about him today. Peter loved going to war and travelled a lot abroad. He also loved his wife, Eleanor of Aragon, and always took her nightdress with him on his travels. But his nobles plotted against him and one night stabbed him in his sleep.

The last Queen of Cyprus was a lady from Venice called Caterina Cornaro, who ruled until the Venetians took over.

Venetian stronghold

Venice was a large maritime empire and the Venetians were very good traders. Cyprus was important to them both for their trade, due to its strategic position on the vital Silk Route to China, and to defend themselves from the Ottomans, who were a growing threat. The Ottomans had already conquered the neighbouring lands and had their eye on Cyprus as well.

The Venetians spent most of the time building defence fortifications around the cities of Nicosia and Famagusta.

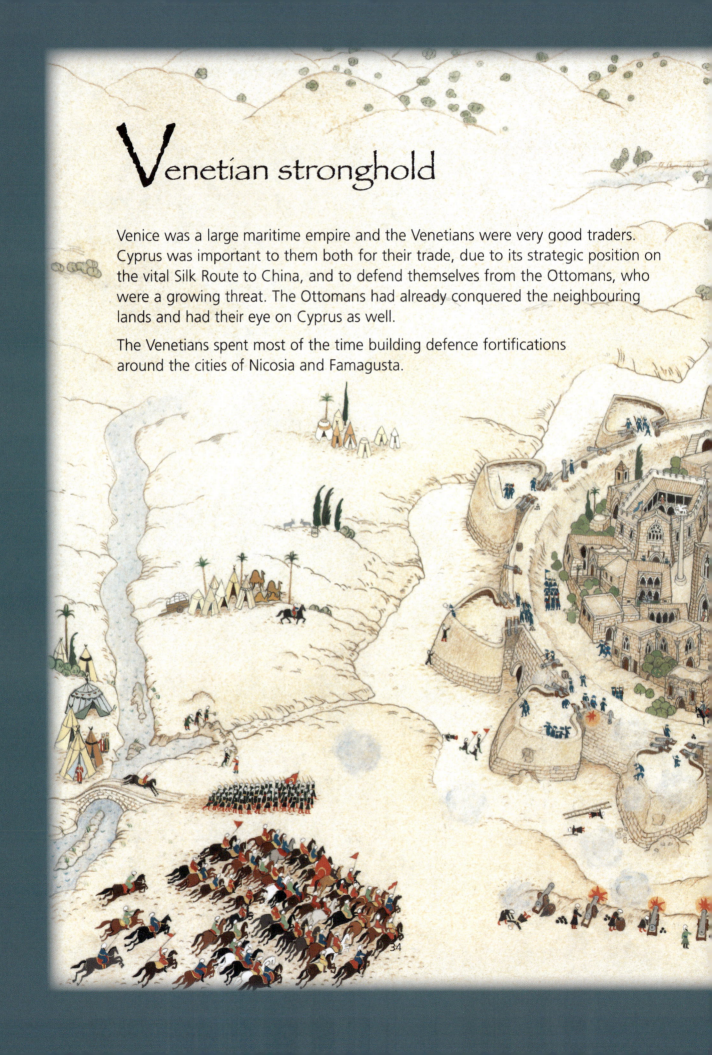

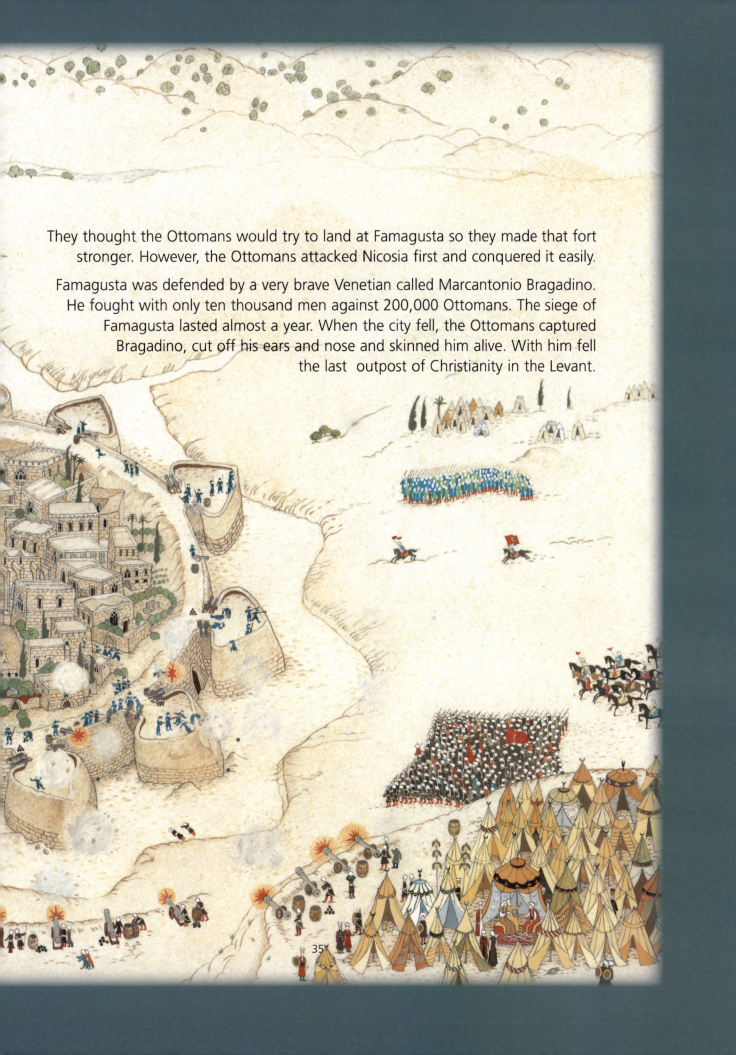

They thought the Ottomans would try to land at Famagusta so they made that fort stronger. However, the Ottomans attacked Nicosia first and conquered it easily.

Famagusta was defended by a very brave Venetian called Marcantonio Bragadino. He fought with only ten thousand men against 200,000 Ottomans. The siege of Famagusta lasted almost a year. When the city fell, the Ottomans captured Bragadino, cut off his ears and nose and skinned him alive. With him fell the last outpost of Christianity in the Levant.

Modern Times

Ottoman rule

The Ottomans ruled Cyprus for 300 years, one of many lands they ruled, known as the Ottoman Empire. Thousands of Ottomans from Turkey settled in Cyprus.

The Sultan in Turkey sent governors to rule Cyprus. They taxed the people heavily. Some Greeks converted to Islam to avoid paying taxes. One pasha, Abu Bekr did many good works, including building an aqueduct to bring water to the town of Larnaca from about six miles away.

The Ottomans abolished serfdom and restored the rights of the Church of Cyprus. They viewed the Archbishop as the leader, or Ethnarch of the Greek community and made him responsible for collecting taxes on their behalf. One important figure at the time was the Dragoman of the Serai (the Governor's Palace), who acted as middleman for all the business between

the Ottomans and the Greek Cypriots. In Turkish, dragoman means translator. One such man was Hadjigeorgakis Kornesios, whose house you can still see in old Nicosia today.

When Greece tried to free itself from Turkish rule during the Greek War of Liberation, which started in 1821, Archbishop Kyprianos of Cyprus helped by sending money and supplies in the hope that Cyprus would be freed too. The Pasha, Mehmed Silahshor, found out what was going on. Archbishop Kyprianos was hanged in the public square in front of the Serai, three bishops' heads were cut off and the Abbot of Kykko and other priests were also killed.

British colony

Cyprus remained under Ottoman rule until 1878 when the Sultan leased the island to Great Britain who later annexed it.

The British ruled Cyprus for 82 years. They built many roads, dams, bridges and hospitals. Cyprus was the first place in the world from where malaria, a disease carried by mosquitoes that live in marshlands, was eradicated, through pesticide spraying and the planting of eucalyptus trees to dry up the marshes. They introduced the British legal system and government, co-operatives and trade unions.

The Greek Cypriots were very pleased to be rid of the Ottomans because they thought the British would help them unite with Greece. But the Turkish Cypriots did not like this idea, which was called *enosis*, afraid that, as they were only about 18% of the population, they would become second class citizens. Later they said there should be *taksim*, or partition, whereby half of Cyprus would go to Greece and the other half to Turkey.

A group of fighters called the National Organisation of Cypriot Fighters (EOKA) was formed led by George Grivas. In 1955 they started a campaign of attacks against the British for *enosis*. The British introduced restrictions on the Greek population and exiled Archbishop Makarios.

In 1959 the Zurich and London Agreements were signed. It was agreed that Cyprus would neither be united with Greece nor divided between Greece and Turkey, but would become independent, which Greece, Turkey and Britain guaranteed. Britain would keep two bases on the island. The President of the new state would be a Greek Cypriot and the Vice-President a Turkish Cypriot. The House of Representatives, the Council of Ministers, the civil service and the police force would be shared between Greek Cypriots and Turkish Cypriots based on a ratio of 7 to 3.

Independence

When the island became an independent republic in 1960, it was the first time in 2,000 years that Cyprus was not ruled by a foreign power. Independence, however, was not without problems.

Cyprus' first President was Archbishop Makarios and its Vice President was Dr Fazil Kuchuck.

Right from the first three years of independence, the Greek and Turkish Cypriot communities started arguing about the constitution. Extremists from both communities revived the issues of *enosis* and partition. The main criticism against Makarios was that he did not do enough to control extremists.

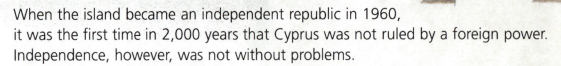

On Christmas Day 1963 fighting broke out and people from both communities were killed.

Then the British intervened in order to keep the two communities from fighting one another. A line in green ink was drawn on a map separating the Greek and Turkish Cypriot areas of Nicosia. This Green Line, as it is known, was first guarded by British troops and then by the United Nations.

The Turkish Cypriot leadership withdrew from the government and, whereas Greek and Turkish Cypriots had previously lived together side by side all over the island, from then on Turkish Cypriots lived mostly in separate enclaves.

Coup, invasion and a plan for peace

On 15 July 1974 the Greek junta staged a *coup d'état to* overthrow President Makarios. Tanks attacked the Presidential Palace in Nicosia but Makarios managed to escape.

Five days later Turkey invaded, saying it had the right to restore the legal government under the Treaty of Guarantee. About a third of the population lost their homes with the Greek Cypriots fleeing to the south and the Turkish Cypriots later moving north. Now the two communities were completely separated with no contact between them taking place. Turkish troops remained even after the rightful government was restored and kept about 40% of the island, including Kyrenia and Famagusta.

In 1983 the northern occupied part of the island was declared independent, but no country in the world except Turkey has recognised it.

Over the years the United Nations tried to help the Greek and Turkish Cypriots find a compromise, which would allow the two communities to live together again in peace. In 2004 they presented the people with a plan to solve the Cyprus problem. Separate referenda were held asking the people if they agreed to the plan. Most of the Turkish Cypriots voted YES but most of the Greek Cypriots voted NO. Shortly afterwards Cyprus joined the European Union but the Cyprus problem was not solved.

Chronology

Ancient Times

8800 - 4000 BC	Neolithic Period
4000 - 2300 BC	Chalcolithic Period
2300 - 1050 BC	Bronze Age
1050 - 750 BC	Geometric Period
750 - 475 BC	Archaic Period
475 - 325 BC	Classical Period
325 - 30 BC	Hellenistic Period
30 BC - 395 AD	Roman Period

The Middle Ages

395 - 1191	Byzantine Period
1192 - 1489	Frankish Period
1489 - 1571	Venetian Period

Modern Times

1571 - 1878	Ottoman Period
1878 - 1960	British Period
1960	Independence

Printed in Poland
by Amazon Fulfillment
Poland Sp. z o.o., Wrocław